Missing Teeth

The Last
Discrimination
Hiding In Plain Sight

Dr. Linda Johnson

ISBN 978-1-0980-7699-3 (paperback)
ISBN 978-1-68570-645-6 (hardcover)
ISBN 978-1-0980-7700-6 (digital)

Christian Faith Publishing, Inc.
832 Park Avenue
Meadville, PA 16335
www.christianfaithpublishing.com

Printed in the United States of America

PRELUDE

Discrimination is the end result of prejudice, racism, and the wielding power of the world's institutions. By institutions, I am referring to the police department, health care system, school system, clothing industry, beauty and cosmetics, and mainstream media. By institutions, I am referring to those giant buildings that seem to have heavy metal doors that are normally locked from the inside. In order to get to the heavy metal doors, you have to climb up a long, winding staircase. These heavy metal doors have a peephole in them. The keeper of the keys can look through the peephole and see who is knocking, trying to get in. The keeper of the keys have the power to let whom they desire inside. Behind the heavy metal doors is a picture on the wall with a perfect smile on it. Anyone who has this perfect smile is granted the rite of passage. The keeper of the keys is the system that has been set in place by the institution that allows one group to enter and, by the same token, locks other groups out.

Over the years, the criteria for the rite of passage has changed—or somewhat shifted. When you make it to the top of the stairs and knock on the door, all you have to do now is present a great big smile. And if your teeth are straight, white, perfect, and are all present, you will hear a big clinging sound. The dead bolt will slide to the left, and the door will open wide for you. It really does not matter what race you are. The only thing you need for a rite of passage is a perfect smile. The keeper of the keys does not care how you got there or what it cost for you to be there. The only important thing is that you showed up with a perfect smile.

It is my desire that the individuals who read this book will go on a journey of self-discovery just like I did. This book is designed for us to understand that our teeth are more important than we realize and that having healthy teeth is the first step toward good health. When I set out to write this book, my thoughts were with the individuals who were suffering in shame and the others who were struggling with the plight of missing teeth. If we adopt the worldview of what perfection looks like, it is a given that some of us will be left out because it is too costly for all of us to fit in. I will not tell you that your teeth have to be perfect. However, I am telling you that your teeth need to be healthy. And that everything you introduce into your body is going to impact your teeth for the good or for the bad. If we do not make our teeth a priority in our youth, they will not be around to serve us in our old age.

I came to the realization that when you write a book you have to be willing to share all of your shortcomings. When you set out to write a book, you have to be willing to be totally vulnerable. Your life becomes an open book when you write a book. And I would hope that in the future, after reading this book, we will be more inclined to have compassion and understanding with individuals who are struggling with their dental issues.

We know that an ounce of prevention is worth a pound of cure. As young parents, let's give our children a running start and bathe them in good oral hygiene at an early age. And hopefully, they too can continue the path to good oral health. While I was growing up, I do not ever remember anyone ever telling me how important my teeth were. Not until I was in my twenties in the military did I receive the grave information. By then, the damage was done. I was not teased in grade school about my teeth; however, we live in a different world now. Children will tease you now, and they will make you feel self-conscious if anything on you just so happens not to be perfect. Hopefully, parents reading this book can give their children a better start than I had.

ACKNOWLEDGMENTS

This book will serve as a dedication to every tooth fairy—real or imagined. Our society will never outgrow its need for a tooth fairy's blessing. All we have to do is look around and there will always be someone who needs our help, love, and encouragement.

So to all the tooth fairies,
we thank you!

Special Thanks

No matter how you live your life, there are always special people who will walk with you hand in hand and arm in arm. I am blessed to have so many people in my life that have helped me and encouraged me and stuck with me on my lifelong journey.

However, when it comes to writing this book, I would like to give special thanks to my best friend in the whole wide world. Her name is Dr. Kathryn Dorn. We have been best friends for over fifty years. And during this journey, she has supported me professionally, and she continues to encourage me.

Dr. Kathryn Dorn assisted me with the editing and proofreading of the manuscript. I owe a lot of gratitude to her for the finished product. And any continued success that I might have is in part due to her support and encouragement.

We both have had a lifelong career together as chemists, quality professionals, toastmasters, Bible college colleagues, and church members. There is no end to the gratitude that I owe Dr. Kathryn Dorn. I can barely remember my life without her being a part of it. I owe so much of my success to her. And I am sure we will continue to do great things together.

My sister, Catherine Beasley, is also due a special thanks. She is the best sister any girl could hope to have. Catherine has always been there for me in all of my lifelong endeavors. During the year that I was writing this book, she encouraged me to complete chapters and meet deadlines. She made sure that I returned phone calls to Dr. Dorn to stay on task. She would ask me every day, "Did you work on your book?" She was so happy when I told her that the publishing company had agreed to publish my book! I would lastly like to thank her for her financial support as well. She is the best!

CONTENTS

FOREWORD

GREGORY YOUNG

Some time ago, I came to know Dr. Johnson through my acquaintance with her sister, who is one of my dearest of friends, the most delightful Catherine Beasley. Their family is known for its academic prowess, ethnic pride, and community service, and charity. And therefore, as I came to know Dr. Johnson as Bobbie Jean, these fine qualities shined upon her as the rising sun and the setting moon. She was for real! At the time, I was wrapping up my readings and research for my master of history degree at Louisiana Tech University. The three of us shared many discussions regarding the current state of affairs with respect to a myriad of subjects: religion, science, sociology, politics, history, entertainment, and yes, sports. It was fun! However, I soon discovered Bobbie Jean was having much more fun than I imagined. Bobbie Jean, that is, Dr. Johnson was undergoing an effort to uncover a secret—one once exposed could unleash powers before unknown to many. She undertook writing a book titled *Missing Teeth: The Last Discrimination Hiding in Plain Sight*.

In writing *Missing Teeth: The Last Discrimination Hiding in Plain Sight*, Dr. Linda Bobbie Johnson brings a megaphone to discuss a topic whose significance is apparent and profound yet is otherwise mentioned below the decibel of a whisper. True to herself, she navigates throughout this neglected arena in terms easily relatable and does so with ease. This fact comes as no surprise to those fortunate enough to really know Dr. Johnson. For this is what she's all about: she has an extraordinary understanding of the potential that lies within things—even the smallest things, neglected things, and yes, the vast potential of a smile.

In fact, her ability to relate to others' pain and potential is central to Dr. Johnson's anthropology, and hereon, her story. The primary focus of her writings—the perils and promises of teeth—embodies Dr. Johnson's personal journey and mission to aid others in their struggles, that they may discover the transcendent powers of a healthy smile in a similar manner as she did.

Dr. Johnson credits her enhanced smile as a critical component in her transformation from what she described as having a "jacked-up and stacked-up mouth" to an accomplished professional in possession of a doctorate. Indeed, she has come a long way from that snaggletoothed little girl playing in the yard to an altruist with hopes of spreading the good news of what adults and children can derive from proper dental care.

Dr. Johnson, as an author, is a true servant in command of a powerful tool. There is much good to be gained from true servants because they are the true masters. For such masters seek not command or control of other people, but rather pursue keys to hand off to those in captive that they may unchain the shackles that bind them. It is my hope that those who read Dr. Johnson's book will come to learn of her story of triumph, and in doing so, learn to free themselves and enjoy the blessings of an enhanced smile.

INTRODUCTION

This book is not meant to be a memoir or an autobiography. I just want to share some vital truths that I have uncovered during my years on this planet. *Missing Teeth: The Last Discrimination Hiding in Plain Sight* is intended to raise awareness to the fact that teeth have a certain power that so many of us are not aware. The reason I want to highlight the discrimination that is hiding in plain sight is because no one will call it that. Discrimination is exactly what it is. So many people are on dead-end jobs because they have jacked-up teeth or missing teeth.

I bring your attention to an elderly woman who works at Walmart all day, just folding clothes, because she has no teeth. The supervisor will not promote her to a position where she will have to interact with the public because she has no teeth. However, they will not say to her, "We would promote you if you had teeth." They will just leave her folding clothes and work around her.

So many of us hide behind our missing teeth. We cannot reflect the life force that is in us via a smile because missing teeth make us self-conscious. And we don't want to be judged unfairly by others, so we hide our smile behind those missing teeth. Missing teeth in our primary years are cute. However, when we progress in age, it is a cloak to be used against us. It is sometimes what corporate America uses to hold us back. The employer wants the best and the brightest to represent their companies and rightfully so. No one will tell you that you need to work on your smile. They will just discriminate against you because of it.

Billions of dollars are spent annually on dental and cosmetic dentistry. Those dollars are spent by the rich who can afford it. The rest of us make do with little or no dental insurance, only going to the dentist to get cheap dentures or extractions of badly infected teeth. As a result, there is a segment of society that goes through life with missing teeth that are caught up in the web of discrimination.

1

Prejudice + Institutional Power = Discrimination

I recently attended the celebration of life of a Jewish matriarch. Among the many things that were said about how she lived her life, I immediately sat up straight in my chair when the rabbi spoke of her activism in the wake of the civil rights movement. It was stated that she abhorred injustice on any level. When she recognized injustice, she fought tooth and nail to address it and to explore the legality of its existence. Here you have a Jewish immigrant that embodies the intended American spirit.

It is impossible to ascertain the frame of mind that the writers and signers of the Declaration of Independence had at the time when life was given to the document. A lot of the men involved owned slaves or knew others that owned slaves. However, the phrase "We hold these truths to be self-evident that all men are created equal. They are endowed by their Creator with certain unalienable rights. That among them are Life, Liberty and the pursuit of Happiness" are mere words with no truth in them to many

Americans who have been shut out of the American dream. So many Americans are no longer dreaming. In fact, they are wide awake. They are wide awake to the reality that mere words on a piece of parchment will not grant us equal rights and equal access to all that this country has to offer.

It has taken me this long to realize that when young people use the word "dis," these are the first three letters of the word *discriminate*. Discrimination always does two things: (1) It allows access to one group and (2) blocks access from another group. It is the access that is involved in the pursuit of happiness alluded to in the Declaration of Independence. And as the United States fought for its independence from Great Britain, minorities fight every day for independence in the United States. If you just explore the rampant discrimination in this nation, there are so many levels until it just gets exhausting. I mean look at the many times that one group of people have recently called law enforcement on another group of people doing ordinary things. It is hard now to be surprised. I mean the sting has almost worn off. But that is a not a good thing. We should never cease to be outraged at prejudicial treatment from others. However, it just gets exhausting. I will not use space to list them here because we are all aware of the many news reports that have invaded our everyday lives. In my mind, that is the worst form of discrimination. When individuals cannot go about their daily lives without being constantly reminded that we need to fear law enforcement.

So when we talk about the last discrimination that is hiding in plain sight, we have not been taught that our level of success and the level of income we can achieve is directly proportional to the smile that we carry everywhere we go. We have not been told that our teeth have capital. We do not realize that there is a price tag on our teeth. Missing teeth will hold us back. We have not been told that missing teeth will block our access to the American dream. Our teeth are our business card. They represent us, and they tell the world everything it needs to know about us.

This is a realization that I discovered all by myself. I just started to look around and listen to people talk about others. I began to pay attention to who was getting promoted, who was getting the big breaks, and who was spending money on teeth. And it just occurred to me one day that teeth just may be the missing link in the whole scheme of things. I started to recognize who was smiling and who wasn't, and I quickly realized that this person was not smiling because of missing teeth. Then I noticed that everyone liked this person or that person because of their beautiful teeth. It was all because of missing teeth or a beautiful white smile. Amazing to me, now that I think of it. I think a big part of it was that nobody wanted to hurt anyone's feelings. Looking back, that might not have been the best path forward. What if the boss told his subordinates that you guys need to make sure you take real good care of your teeth? That might have made a difference.

My first notion that my teeth were important to me came during the six years I spent in the army. The mental health official told us that, as soldiers, it was very important that we get our teeth cleaned twice a year and that we needed to make sure that our teeth got the best of care because we cannot be combat ready if we had toothaches.

He told us that we cannot subdue the enemy if the enemy was in our mouth. I took that as a clue that my teeth were mission essential, and from that day forward, I became very conscious about my teeth. That was the military. That civilian boss is just like your college professor, he/she is not going to tell you what you should and should not do. They expect you to be adults on the job. However, you don't know what you don't know. So many of us are unconscientiously incompetent when it comes to the value of our teeth. If we knew that there was a monetary value attached to our teeth, we would surely take better care of them. If we knew that society will use our missing teeth to hold us back, we would replace missing teeth. If we knew that the amount of money we could make is tied to our smile, we would probably take better care of our teeth.

What do missing teeth tell us about a person? If you ever watch the evening news when the roving reporter is on location, I don't know how they manage to do it, but every time they interview a member of the community regarding the crime that has just been committed, the person that they choose to place in front of the camera almost always have teeth missing. I don't know why that is. I think the reason is because so many of the people in the community have missing teeth. There are so many things that missing teeth tell us about a person. Missing teeth tell us that the individual probably does not have dental insurance. Or that the individual does not have the money to pay for dental services that are not covered by dental insurance. Or that the individual does not know the value of his smile. Or that the individual is just okay with missing teeth. Culturally, missing teeth are not a problem in most communities. Poverty-stricken communities are okay with individuals with missing teeth. Because we understand that not everyone has access to affordable dental care. However, the real world is not that forgiving. The real world will judge you if you have missing teeth. The real world will treat you with contempt if you have missing teeth. The fact of the matter is that society does not give allowances for missing teeth. The last discrimination hiding in plain sight—missing teeth will hold you back. Missing teeth will decrease your face value. Missing teeth tell the world that you probably are a drug user, a prolonged smoker, or an alcoholic. Missing teeth tell the world that you just got teeth extracted and not replaced. Missing teeth tell the world that, at some point, you neglected to take care of the teeth that you once had. Because all of us had twenty-five to thirty-two teeth at one time. Missing teeth tell the world that you are okay with missing teeth. Missing teeth tell the world that you do not care that the world is judging you by your missing teeth. Get over my missing teeth and that I spend my money on whatever it is that I choose to spend it on.

It is not good manners to stare at someone's open mouth. However, when a person talks, we readily see the condition of their teeth. It is incumbent upon us not to judge so harshly individuals with missing teeth unless we are in a position to help them. Even if you told some of them, they would be just ok with their missing teeth.

Why are teeth a priority? Because a full set of teeth say to the world that you are complete. They indicate that you care about what others think of you and that you want to put your best foot forward. A healthy smile says that you have prepared yourself for success. And that you can be trusted. A full set of teeth say to the world that you are healthy, friendly, that you love life, a healthy eater and are living.

The United States Constitution does not directly address employment discrimination. However, the Fifth and Fourteenth Amendments to the United States Constitution limit the power of the federal and state governments to discriminate. The Fifth Amendment has an explicit requirement that the federal government does not deprive individuals of "life, liberty, or property," without due process of the law. It also contains an implicit guarantee that the Fourteenth Amendment explicitly prohibits states from violating an individual's rights of due process and equal protection. However, federal law governing employment discrimination has developed over time. Title VII of the Civil Rights Act of 1964 created the Equal Employment Opportunity Commission (EEOC) to administer the judicial ramification of the Civil Rights Act. Title VII prohibits discrimination based on race, color, religion, sex, or national origin. Under federal law, employers cannot discriminate against employees or prospective employees on the basis of race, sex, pregnancy, religion, national origin, disability, age, military service, bankruptcy, genetic information, or citizenship status. The aforementioned list is what we call a protected class. This means that Title VII makes it illegal for employers to discriminate based upon protected characteristic regarding terms, conditions, and privileges of employment.

Since it is now against the law to discriminate against an individual on the basis of their race, creed, gender, sexual orientation, and age, the human race is finding more new subtle ways to discriminate. By discrimination, we use the following formula: prejudice + institutional power = discrimination. For years, we have been using obesity as our target for discrimination.

Discrimination is when someone treats you differently, unfairly based on characteristics that you cannot change. These certain obvious characteristics have been placed in a protected class. In other words, the law is going to protect you from being unlawfully judged based on characteristics that you cannot change, such as your race, your heritage, your age, your sex/gender. Because there is implicit bias in individuals, discrimination will still exist.

Employers are bound by law not to discriminate on the basis of race, creed, gender, age, sexual orientation. There is another low-hanging fruit that is right there in plain sight every time we interview for a job and smile. Anytime someone wants to hold you back, they will find a way. Thanks to the drug culture, rampant poverty, and just poor oral hygiene, we have handed corporate America all the ammunition it needs in order to discriminate against a whole class of people. These people are talented, smart, bright, and very much in need of comparable employment. However, because they have missing teeth, employers can reserve the right not to hire them or not to promote them.

If someone told you when you were in your teens that your teeth might determine how much money you could make, you probably would have taken better care of them.

If you knew that smoking cigarettes, drinking sodas, using drugs would jeopardize your future income, you probably would have done a lot of things differently.

There are many articles on the web that share comments from Malcolm Gladwell, a social scientist, about how bad teeth have power to impact how people are treated. I found it intriguing that he believes the condition of one's teeth will be the next wave of discrimination trending toward becoming the new standard of inequality. His views further solidify my thoughts that missing teeth will greatly impact your chance of landing a prized job when compared to other applicants with a full set of polished teeth.

I think what we are missing is the fact that it's not really about the teeth. It's also the fact that the individual didn't care enough about themselves to get their teeth fixed.

It is a proven fact that people with bad teeth, unfortunately, are often refused certain entry-level jobs, thus immediately predisposing them to a reduced chance of success. Malcolm Gladwell states that comparing the bad state of teeth to obesity are essentially one and the same because they indicate the same type of subtle discrimination.

We often focus on race and ethnicity as the great dividers in American society, but in reality, we would argue that race and ethnicity differences are secondary to class today as the great divider. The author, Sarah Smarsh, tells the story of teeth far better than any we have ever heard.

Inequalities in oral health and dental access reflect our deepest social and economic divides. Ashamed and stigmatized, the poor are shut out of opportunities for social advancement as well as work that could help them escape poverty. If you have lousy teeth, you can't get a job in some disciplines. The Hollywood smile has become a status symbol around the world and better off Americans routinely pay for elective procedures ranging from teeth whitening and veneers to complete smile makeovers costing many thousands of dollars. Meanwhile, more than one out of three low-income American adults avoid smiling because of poor oral health.

The struggle over the recognition of health care as a human right has been a long one in the United States. Yet often, when dental services have been mentioned at all, they have remained a marginal part of the debate. However, this may be changing. In 2000, the then U.S. Surgeon General David Satcher reframed dental disease as oral disease, and oral disease as a public health crisis. In his landmark oral health in America report, Satcher warned that from cavities to gum disease to oral cancers, a silent epidemic was raging in our own nation. Those who suffer the worst oral health are found among the poorest of all ages with poor children and poor older Americans particularly vulnerable. Members of racial and ethnic minority groups also experience a disproportionate level of oral health problems. Satcher urged recognition of the fact that oral health and general health are inseparable.

Since its beginnings as a profession in 1840, with the opening of the world's first dental college in Baltimore, dentistry has evolved in isolation from the rest of the nation's health care system. Our heads may be attached to our bodies, but generations of dental and medical providers have been educated separately. They work in different worlds, and many patients get lost in between.

An individual applied for a job at a well-known theme park. The interview was going well until she smiled broadly, then suddenly the interviewer said that she could not hire her because she was missing a side front tooth. She told the individual that when she got her tooth fixed, she could reapply. The young lady mentioned the incident to a current employee and was told that it was total discrimination. According to attorneys from Chicago, Florida, New York, and California, the incident is not discrimination. Gender, race, age, religion, and sexual orientation are forms of workplace discrimination. Good or bad dental hygiene is not a protected class.

Studies show that bad teeth prevent otherwise qualified candidates from getting jobs or promotions. Although the US is on the cutting edge of innovations in dentistry, many Americans have poor oral health and crooked or missing teeth. Many don't go to the dentist because they do not have insurance and can't afford to pay out of pocket for dental care. The scope of the problem is widespread. Close to one-half of Americans are without dental insurance according to data from the Department of Health and Human Services. Access to dental care is limited in two basic ways. First, many don't have health insurance. And second, there is a shortage of dentists who are willing to treat the poor.

Earlier in the year (2019), the managers of a counseling firm were struggling to fill a position at their front desk. They blazed through a string of potential candidates sent by the staffing agency, but none of the candidates had the qualifications they were looking for in a future employee. And then the agency sent Brenda (not her real name), a thirty-five-year-old mother of three who entered the workforce after her husband was laid off from his factory job. Everyone in the office loved Brenda and thought that she would fit in. Later the staff learned at the company meeting that they hired someone else. When asked why, the boss replied that Brenda had bucked teeth, and her teeth were crocked. The boss said it wasn't the image that the company wanted to project at the firm.

This is not an isolated incident. Studies show that bad teeth prevent otherwise qualified candidates from getting good jobs and promotions. Although bad teeth cause unpleasant oral issues, such as gingivitis, periodontal disease, speech disorders, the consequences go beyond physical health and often costs psychological well-being in most individuals. Bad teeth dampen your spirit. And some of us with bad teeth have to live with this gloom every day of our lives, especially since it cannot be fixed overnight.

Teeth are the first thing we notice about an individual. First of all, it is extremely hard to find a dating partner if you have missing teeth or crocked teeth. I am told that missing teeth are a game changer in the dating scene. And many of us are instantly attracted to someone with a healthy set of teeth.

Society tends to judge individuals unfairly when they have missing teeth. When we do this, we give teeth the power to have a strong impact on our daily lives. Now that this unfair treatment due to missing teeth has been brought to your attention, what will you do about it?

2

Missing Teeth and the Butterfly Effect

Small changes good or bad can result in big differences, which is, in essence, the butterfly effect. The minute a person breaks a bad habit, overall health starts to improve. Since the mouth is the gateway to nutrition, we must become aware that everything we eat, drink, and chew impacts our teeth in a good way or in a bad way.

An American meteorologist by the name of Edward N. Lorenz (1917–2008) invented the concept of the butterfly effect. If you notice that when the butterfly flaps its wing, their bodies contract. As the body of the butterfly contracts, this particular motion pushes a current of air under its wings. This is how the butterfly advances itself in the air. The butterfly is actually propelled through the air by the flapping of its wings. This propelling motion allows the butterfly to make contact with the environment. To the naked eye this looks effortless on the part of the butterfly. Almost as if the butterfly gently glides through the air automatically with no effort or intention. According to Edward N. Lorenz, the butterfly effect is a small thing; however, studies have been shown to prove that the slightest changes in the environment downstream can have grave consequences upstream. Signifying that the butterfly flapping its wings do not actually cause the change in weather dynamics or weather patterns, but the action of its wings flapping causes a disturbance in the interconnected complex web that holds the whole universe together.

I use the analogy of the butterfly effect to demonstrate the fact that everything we eat, chew, or drink in our early years will impact our teeth in our latter years. If you look at individuals in their younger years, their teeth are all present, white, and strong. However, when you fast-forward twenty or thirty years in the future, that same individual's teeth are missing, tarnished, crocked, cracked, chipped, or gone all together. My question is: How can this be? What happened? Using the butterfly effect, it is a gradual thing. We wake up one morning, and we look in the mirror, and we are saddened by the smile that is looking back at us.

Any major event in history can be traced to one small occurrence can demonstrate the butterfly effect. Look at the sinking of the Titanic on April 14, 1912. I have watched several documentaries on the investigative reports as to what actually caused the Titanic to sink. However, based on all of the research that the different engineers and designers have been able to put together in order to give us a clear picture as to what actually happened the night that the Titanic sank, the one piece of documentary that stands out in my mind is that the Titanic would have sunk even if there were no icebergs in the ocean. Apparently, ten days before the ship's scheduled departure a fire began in one of the coal bunkers and continued to burn for several days into the voyage. Now I had no idea what a coal bunker was when I first saw the documentary. However, Google defines a coal bunker as a storage for coal awaiting use or transportation. This can be for use in domestic, commercial, or on a ship or a locomotive.

If we would just look at the Holocaust, this bears a resemblance of another example of the butterfly effect. As atrocious as it is, it was birth in the mind of Hitler because of one incidence. In the early nineteen hundreds, a young Hitler applied for art school and was rejected, possibly by a Jewish professor. By his own estimation and that of scholars, this rejection went on to shape his metamorphosis from an aspiring bohemian artist into the human manifestation of evil. We can only speculate as to how history would have been different.

I was working at a country and western radio station on January 28, 1986 on that fateful morning when the shuttle exploded, seventy-three seconds after it launched, killing everyone onboard. Our station historian and statistician was so devastated by the event, he had a heart attack and died sitting in his recliner watching the news reports. It was nine o'clock, and he had not come to work yet. We phoned his house, and there was no answer. We sent two disc jockeys to his house to check on him. They found him, deceased in his recliner with the television still on. We surmised what had happened.

Investigators found that a faulty design on O-rings, a type of gasket, caused a leak in one of the two rocket boosters that ignited the shuttles fuel tank. No one predicted the low temperatures of the launch day. It was discovered that the low temperatures stiffened the rubber O-rings so much so that they could not maintain a seal in the joint that, because of poor design, opened the gap that the rings were supposed to seal during the first second after ignition, giving a secure ride into outer space.

The butterfly effect is demonstrated by individuals who abuse alcohol and do not follow a dental hygiene ritual. We have to be very careful. Our teeth are always the victims. They are always the innocent bystanders. There are so many articles on the internet with excerpts from different studies that highlight, "without good oral hygiene, the regular use of alcohol can have an adverse effect on teeth and gums and can cause significant tooth damage." It can also cause dry mouth and tooth erosion. Dry mouth is a condition where the flow of saliva is reduced and this condition increases the risk of tooth decay.

More dental reviews and studies from the internet document other drugs that carry a high risk to your oral health include marijuana, cocaine, ecstasy, heroin, methamphetamine, cigarettes, and tobacco. Marijuana is known to cause dry mouth, which can lead to an increased risk of gum problems. Continuous use of cocaine when mixed with a person's saliva can create an acidic solution that erodes tooth enamel. Cocaine and another form of it called crack is also known to cause dry mouth. Prolonged use of ecstasy (love drug) produces side effects, such as tooth grinding, jaw clenching, and dry mouth. Heroin users tend to crave sweet foods, which can increase the risk of tooth decay if dental hygiene is neglected. Heroin can also cause dry mouth and tooth grinding. Methamphetamine (speed, ice, or meth) is cited as the drug that causes severe tooth decay in a very short time period because of its acidic properties that can attack tooth enamel. We are all well-versed on the many ways smoking is harmful to the human body. However, the research hardly ever mentions the many ways smoking adversely affects the teeth. Tobacco products, whether smoked or chewed, are known to cause gum problems. Recent studies on e-cigarettes use reveals how they trigger an inflammatory response in gum tissues. The alarming effect of the drug culture plays a role in oral health issues, such as bone loss, tooth loss, dry mouth, bad breath, tooth decay, and periodontal diseases. In many people, this is a gradual process that takes place over many years, and if detected and treated, can be halted.

In America, we have an oral health crisis that the drug culture has played its parts, by and large, due to the laws and legislation that our elected officials have allowed to run rampant in this country. Why is it that Medicare will pay for dentures and not tooth replacement? This bears some investigation. When we look at the butterfly effect, we must take responsibility for the part we, as adults, played in this oral health crisis drama. We put more effort into looking good than we do on oral health. We did not include dental health into our overall physical health. We thought that our way of life would not impact our oral health.

Michelle Obama in her book *Becoming* on page nine, described the piano in which she took music lessons on as reminding her of a person with bad teeth. Simply because some of the keys were missing. Also, some of the keys were chipped, damaged, and tarnished. Some of us use our teeth to tear open packages and chop ice, and we bite our finger-nails. Teeth were never designed to do those things.

My own personal family life demonstrates the butterfly effect. Reflecting on my early years as a mother, I wanted to make sure that my two sons had everything they needed in order to lay hold of the American dream. That included teaching them to avoid a life of drug use and providing the resources for the best and brightest smile they could wear. Having said that, I knew how important it was for them to have heathy, straight, white teeth. I knew the tide had turned and that we were living in a culture where they would not be given a pass for having bad or missing teeth. They both got braces in the tenth grade and got them off by graduation. The orthodontist advised me to wait until they were tenth grade because their jaw structures were still forming. So I did as he advised. When my youngest son got his braces off, the people at church indicated to me that his teeth looked like false teeth. I now see the subtle dis-crimination in that. They were essentially saying that they had not seen individuals with straight, white teeth. The only teeth they had seen like that were dentures. And when he started getting compliments about his teeth, he gained a level of confidence, and it gave him a sense of pride in himself.

We just excused the fact that Grandmama did not have teeth or that she had false teeth. I remember the first time my youngest son saw my mother's false teeth in a glass by her bed. He came running to tell me that Grandmama's teeth were out of her mouth. He was traumatized because he had not seen teeth anywhere but in a person's mouth.

It was a shock to him to find out that teeth could actually come out of a person's mouth like that.

It is funny now that I think of it. But that is the reality of a culture where teeth were extracted and not replaced. Or a culture where old age and dentures went hand in hand. A culture where an entire generation of Black folks went to the dentist to get extractions and dentures. And to the credit of the dentist, he did extract the teeth in order to improve the health of the patient.

The cheapest and most important thing you can give a person is your smile. A smile means that I have invited someone else to be a part of me. I have allowed someone else to be a part of my private space. And it lets another person know that the space where I am is safe to come into. Therefore, they feel an instant connection with me. And if my smile is beautiful, healthy, wholesome, with no teeth missing, then I have won someone into my confidence. Sometimes we find ourselves so reluctant to smile because we know that we will be judged severely by the declining condition of our teeth. We negate to show our true selves because of the condition of our teeth.

Remember drug dependence or drug use that causes the person to neglect their personal hygiene, diet, and dental care can significantly increase the risk of dental problems. When this happens, we set ourselves up for all kinds of pain, anguish, and eventually loss of teeth. This could be prevented if we would just maintain a regular oral hygiene routine. It is very important that we brush our teeth twice a day (morning and night). Get regular dental check-ups and limit sugar, alcohol, coffee, cola, and drugs.

In studying the butterfly effect, we come to the realization that there are no isolated events. We realize that every event gives rise to another occurrence. Every weather pattern, every cold front, every heat wave, and every avalanche—all of these events start downstream and materialize upstream.

The use of drugs, the abuse of alcohol, eating sweets, and not having a regular oral health routine will result in an adverse effect on your oral health. History itself holds the clues to these connections. However, we have to embrace history enough for her to give us the underlying causes of times and events.

3

The Tooth Fairy

When we think of the tooth fairy, we think of innocent times when missing teeth represented hope and possibly fairness of the new life ahead for a child. However, if we do not take very good care of those "god" teeth, the tooth fairy will visit us later on, but in a not-so-innocent and forgiving way. I often see little children at church with loose teeth. I know that before too long, that tooth that is just hanging by a thread is gradually moving out of the way for the permanent teeth to come in and announce itself. Because when we see the "god" tooth getting loose, we know that there is a permanent tooth just waiting underneath that tooth to make its arrival.

However, there is a different finality to the loose tooth when we become adults. We understand that when we lose teeth as adults, new teeth are not going to grow back. Teeth don't repair themselves like other body organs because teeth are made of enamel. This enamel is the hardest substance in the entire human body. Teeth don't contain many proteins and cells, which are present in abundant supply in other parts of the body. All throughout your body, cells are being replaced and regenerated. With every breath you take, you introduce 10^{22} atoms into your body. These atoms help our bodies replace and regenerate itself. Radioactive isotopes show that in less than one year, we replace all the atoms in our bodies. We make a new liver in about six weeks; a new stomach lining every five days; new skin once a month; a new skeleton every three months. All of our brain cells are constantly being replaced. However, tooth enamel will not be replaced in your body. Scientists cannot grow tooth enamel in vitro. Teeth have to be replaced by dentists. Modern-day dental implants are made of titanium alloy, which is highly biocompatible. An alloy is a substance made by melting two or more elements together, where at least one of them is a metal. An alloy crystalizes upon cooling into a solid solution, mixture, or intermetallic compound. The components of alloys cannot be separated using physical means. In other words, left undisturbed, alloys remain intact forever. Examples of common alloys: steel which is a combination of iron (metal) and carbon (non-metal); bronze, a combination of copper (metal) and tin (metal); brass is a combination of copper (metal) and zinc (metal). However, prosthetic components of the implants are still made from gold alloys, stainless steel, cobalt-chromium, and nickel chromium alloys.

In March of 2019, I paid $4200 for two implants. That was just for the roots. I paid another $1600 for the crowns. The oral surgeon did the actual root implants; and the dentist did the crowns. The dentist will call and make you an appointment so that they can actually match the crown hue to your present teeth. And when you get finished with this process, the implants blend in with your own teeth. Amazing! The roots are very expensive. However, the outcome is amazing. You walk away with two new, state-of-the-art teeth. The dentist and oral surgeon are now your tooth fairies, and they don't leave gifts under your pillow. No, they don't even send you a bill because you pay for all of their services up-front with either cash or credit card.

Dental implants costs are expensive, but dental implants are not expensive. How does that make sense? Well, when considering the return for the investment that you'll get from securing a healthy, functional, and beautiful smile, the cost is justified. It's important to understand that a dental implant is not a simple piece of equipment. The materials and tools that are able to restore teeth are of incredible quality and cost a lot to make. First, a piece of pure titanium is precisely shaped into a screw form for the implant to be fixed into the jaw bone. Titanium may not be an expensive material, but the process of refining and crafting it is. It doesn't just end with titanium though. All dental implants require a uniquely designed crown to be placed on top of the titanium screw. Everyone has different teeth; no two dental crowns can be the same, which means that dentists cannot mass-produce the crowns. Each crown has to be specifically designed for each patient after the dentist evaluates their mouth and what kind of shape they require. The material used to make the crowns is not very expensive, but the process of molding the crown to create a 3D model and then casting the crown is expensive. So yes, the materials and tools used in the whole process do raise the dental implants cost, but without the specific materials and the tools, the longevity, effectiveness, and quality of the implant are all affected.

Another factor to consider is the team involved in the process of restoring your smile. Dental implants cost also includes the cost associated with your dentist's skill and expertise in creating the implant and crown as well as securing it into your jawbone. Both the procedure of fixing the screw and placing the crown over the screw are very complicated and require an immense amount of precision and detail—a skill dentists have worked very hard and long hours to acquire. Lastly, they have to ensure the implant allows full and normal functionality of your mouth with routine check-ups and working out any complications (if there are any).

Given all these factors, dental implants aren't actually expensive; they are simply high-cost for very valid and valuable reasons (as discussed above). However, this isn't to say that there aren't affordable options—rather true costs—for dental implants. By the time I completed my process of securing two implants, I had spent a total of $4200 for the roots and $1600 for the crowns—a total of $5800. And this was all out of pocket. Dental insurance does not cover the cost of implants. There are too many Americans who cannot afford this kind of out-of-pocket expense. That is why we see so many Americans with missing teeth, both male and female.

There are two instances that I read about, where dental services were, for some reason, out of reach. The first one occurred in February 2007, involving a twelve-year-old by the name of Demonte Driver. He could have used a tooth fairy. Demonte Driver needed only $80 for a tooth extraction which would have saved his life. Every time you go to the dentist, I want you to remember his name. His death was so tragic and so preventable. It saddens my heart that he fell victim to a heartless system that would allow a twelve-year-old to meet such a tragic death in the wealthiest nation in the whole world.

The second instance was about Kyle Willis, who was a twenty-four-year-old male without a job and no health or dental insurance. He could have used a tooth fairy also. We never outgrow our need for a tooth fairy. In August of 2011, this young man had a mere toothache, but due to no dental insurance, he could not have the procedure done to extract the infected wisdom tooth. Weeks later, he was stricken with a headache, then later, his face became swollen. As you can see, his condition was getting progressively worse. By this time, he finds himself in the emergency room. The doctors prescribe painkillers and antibiotics. With no job and no dental insurance, he could not afford $3 for painkillers and $27 for the antibiotics. He opted to buy the painkillers for $3. Since he did not buy the antibiotics, the infection just ran rampant throughout his body and eventually spread to his brain, making him delirious. Not being able to find a tooth fairy to rescue him, he later died. I read this story in horror. How can this be? According to the Kaiser Family Foundation, "For every one adult without health insurance, there are three without dental insurance." They also found that one in four adults has untreated tooth decay and that low-income adults are twice as likely as other adults to have this illness. Our health care crisis is purely economics.

Here you have two grave incidents where simple solutions were available; however, neither individual had access to the information that would have ultimately saved their lives. Had Kyle Willis simply gotten the antibiotics instead of the pain medication, his infection would have cleared up. And if Kyle Willis only knew that the hospital had a dental service connected to it for individuals who were not insured, he could have gotten the medical attention that he needed in order to prevent his untimely death. We have to figure out a way to inform the general public that there is help available if they ask the right questions or inquire of the right source.

Those of us who are privy to information and resources have to be the tooth fairy to the general public that is not aware of the resources available. We have to be the tooth fairy to individuals who are struggling with dental care issues and have no place to turn. It is incumbent upon us to be the tooth fairy in situations that we know about, involving individuals who are seeking to improve their smile or who just need support with dental hygiene issues. When I needed the $1600 for my two crowns, my sister gave me $900 because I was tapped out at that point. When I went to the oral surgeon to get an appointment for cost and time and all of the procedures involved in the process, the receptionists did not inform me that I could get a CareCredit card designed specifically for dental services. When I discussed it with my best friend, she informed me of the CareCredit card. I applied and was instantly approved for

$3000 credit. When I went back for my appointment, I asked them why they did not tell me that I could apply for the CareCredit card. They were absolutely clueless. Just to illustrate the fact that if we do not connect ourselves with individuals who have resources or who have not had similar experiences, we will be forever in the dark. It would be nice if the dental community would do better at informing us of what is available to us. And when I got the CareCredit card in the mail and went back for my appointment, I noticed the logo on the wall at the oral surgeon's office. And since I have used all of my benefits for 2019, I am waiting for 2020 to roll around so that I can get one last tooth replaced with either a crown, bridge, or an implant.

The appeal is, "Who can I be a tooth fairy to by simply sharing knowledge or other resources?"

4

Teeth and Television

I am a stargazer, not at the stars in the sky, but the stars on the big screen. I am always drawn to people's teeth first and their smile second. I can remember the first time I saw Denzel Washington on television or in a movie. I loved his teeth and his smile. One Sunday evening, while living in North Little Rock, Arkansas, I was visiting the home of my best friend. We saw a special on Denzel Washington. The commentator mentioned the fact that his producers recognized his talent and had his teeth perfected. They knew that he was worth the investment. Although, if you watch the movie, *Roman J. Israel, Esq.*, the caps were taken off his teeth in order to be plausible so that he would look exactly like the leading role. He was fantastic.

I remember the line in the movie, *What's Love Got to Do with It*, when Ike looked in Tina's mouth and told her that he was going to send her to his dentist to get her teeth checked out. He knew the impact that teeth would have on her future success as an entertainer.

Fantasia has a beautiful set of teeth. When she sings, she opens her mouth wide and the melody flows from her soul. You can see everything in her mouth. And from what I can see, her teeth are perfect.

Tyler Perry has a great set of teeth. Madea's (his stage character) teeth are just perfect. They are white, pearly, straight, and just beautiful. She uses all the talent that she has when she brings you into her living room. I love to see him/her smile.

Trevor Noah, in my opinion, has the best smile on television. He is so cute, with that award-winning smile. I know that people join in four nights a week just to see that smile and those teeth. Steve Harvey is another one of my absolute favorites. He has the whitest teeth. He smiles for the camera when he hosts *Family Feud*. I notice how the cameraman will come in and get a close-up of those white teeth of his.

Robin Roberts has a healthy set of teeth. She has an engaging smile. She makes you feel warm and comfy when she smiles. Oprah's teeth say that I like you when she smiles. Her teeth are beautiful. I like the sound of her voice. Paula Patton has nice teeth. I really noticed them in the movie, *Idlewild*, when she was singing at the church. Tyrese and Regina King have nice teeth. Regina King has a healthy smile. She smiles so freely. Every day at 5:30 p.m., I watch Lester Holt. He has a commanding voice. He only smiles at the end when he does the segment on *Inspiring America*. His teeth are nice and rich-looking.

Chris Rock is an amazing actor. He has starred in several films and has hosted the Oscars. In 1997, he starred in the action Film *Lethal Weapon*. Also starring in this movie were Danny Glover, Mel Gibson, and my all-time favorite

Joe Peshi. After his movie debut in *Lethal Weapon*, Chris Rock spent all of his proceeds on a mouth makeover. This was indeed a wise investment. $150,000 represented his total earnings for this movie (just to illustrate the importance teeth played in his career). This was a wise investment for him. Look at how it has paid off for the rest of his career.

George Clooney has a history of teeth grinding. By grinding the teeth, they become shorter. So George Clooney got white veneers to lengthen his sparkling smile.

Morgan Freeman is no doubt a gifted actor and artist. However, his teeth had yellowed as he aged. The Oscar nominee had them whitened and also had the gap in the middle filled. Now he has that perfect Hollywood smile.

Miley Cyrus has had some serious dental work in the last few years. The pop star revealed that she had gotten veneers in last couple of years. You can see how they add face value to her smile.

When you see these people on television and on the big screen, you cannot help but notice how perfect, straight, and white their teeth are. Tom Cruise is one of my favorite movie stars. I don't think he has ever starred in a movie that I didn't see at least twice. The pretty white, straight teeth make them look trustworthy, authentic, and healthy. You are captivated by their smile, and you want them to succeed. Have you ever noticed that the good guys always have good teeth and the villain always have bad teeth, missing teeth, or stained teeth? The villain always has teeth that you do not trust. Do you see how the entertainment industry has communicated these subtle messages to us for so long?

I think I may have mentioned earlier that Denzel Washington has caps on his teeth. However, he removed them in order to play Roman J. Israel, Esq.

Roman J. Israel, Esq. was a legal savant who spent decades in a firm's back office. In the film, there is a visible gap between his two front teeth, and he rarely smiles.

I was living in Kernersville, North Carolina, when Fantasia won *America Idol* in 2004. I had not heard of her prior to this event. I found out later that she was actually from High Point, North Carolina. This was so exciting to me. By 2008, she further improved on her smile getting braces to make her smile even brighter and straighter. Evidently, the people with whom she surrounds herself enlightened her on the importance of making her teeth look as white and as straight as possible.

You will never see a greater set of teeth than those in Tyler Perry's mouth. He has the brightest, straightest, most perfect set of teeth that I have ever seen. I can't find anywhere in any search engine where he has ever had any work done on his teeth. They are just perfect. That is why, when Madea smiles, you know that you will absolutely enjoy the movie.

Will Smith's smile is contagious. Even when he messes up and tricks someone, you don't get upset with him because he has such a great smile.

I just finished watching *The General's Daughter* starring Leslie Ann Stefanson as Captain Elizabeth Campbell, the general's daughter. Her teeth are just pearly white. I just noticed them for the second time. She is just beautiful. When she smiles wide, and the light reflects off of her teeth, it looks as if she has pearls glistening in her mouth.

The commonality here is that all of these TV personalities and movie stars have invested in themselves wisely; from face-lifts to body sculpting, to hair and makeup. They knew in order to get the fame, fortune, and a star on the Hollywood Walk of Fame, their teeth had to represent to the world the person on the inside. It is sad to say that our teeth are a mild representation of who we are and who we aspire to be. However, I am finding a trend here. Educated people invest in their teeth. Rich people invest in their teeth. People who place a high premium on their self-worth and their self-image invest in their teeth. They not only invest in their teeth, but also their children's teeth. I am not advocating that to have beautiful teeth, you need to be rich and famous. You don't have to be rich in order to look rich. I am just suggesting that in order for you to be plausible, you need to look the part. People will respect you more when you respect yourself.

5

The Evolution of Teeth

The human race has evolved from eating whatever we could catch, kill, grow, and anything we could gather in the wild. If you look at the animal kingdom, the purpose of teeth varies differently across the spectrum. Lower forms of animals use their teeth mainly to fight, fetch, and chew. Whereas, humans basically use their teeth to chew and grind food. Prehistoric men didn't have processed food, so their teeth were bigger, stronger, and farther apart. As the diet of humans changed and evolved, so did the purpose of teeth. When we look at the evolution of teeth, we no longer use our teeth as tools for heavy grinding or tearing food during the eating process.

Now our teeth are more seen as a status symbol. Straight, white, and healthy-looking teeth are out of reach for so many Americans. Too many contend with the stigma of missing teeth, stained, chipped, or diseased teeth. In this age of impressionism, teeth are now associated readily with our socioeconomic level.

We have evolved into an era where having white teeth has become an important aspect of looking our best. I remember when a person's smile used to be just a facial expression. Now it is a statement about who you are. The smile is the first thing people notice about another person. Therefore, replacing missing teeth is highly advised.

Most of us have heard the story of George Washington's teeth. For those of you who haven't, there is a long-standing theory that in his later years, he had dentures made of wood. Although this is a popular rumor, George Washington's teeth were not in fact constructed from wood. In actuality, they were made of several materials such as ivory, gold, and lead. Even though his teeth were not made of wood, his dentures caused him some degree of pain. He complained that they were ill-fitting, uneasy in the mouth, and caused his lips to bulge out. Last but not least, they worked themselves loose.

Today modern dentistry has made leaps and bounds since the day of our first president, from state-of-the-art lasers to the most technologically-advanced dental procedures. Cosmetic dentistry can vastly improve just about anyone's oral health and the appearance of their teeth if they can afford it.

Replacing missing teeth literally makes the face appear more youthful. When missing teeth are not replaced, the individual is very likely to experience facial bone loss as time progresses. This can alter the shape of the face, making the jaw appear smaller. Your teeth are the gateway to good nutrition. Missing just one tooth can cause the neighboring teeth to drift into the space and the opposing tooth drop down. If left untreated, the bite can collapse in just a few years.

Teeth in the back are designed to grind up the food and make it into small pieces that are easy to absorb and digest in the gastrointestinal and the gut. The front teeth start the process of tearing the food, and the tongue directs the food backward to be further crushed and compacted by the larger back molars, readied with the enzymes in the saliva for swallowing. The more time the teeth are used to mash up food, the easier it is for the stomach to pick up the nutrients and vitamins from food. That is why it is very important that we replace missing teeth. However, that effort can be very costly.

Your teeth also help you talk and contribute to your personal appearance. Speech is affected by the way the teeth meet, the movement of the jaw, and the movement of the tongue around the teeth. Appearance is affected by the bite of the teeth and the bones surrounding them. Missing teeth, crowding, or the size of the jaw bones may cause the teeth to line up in the wrong way. These problems and tooth loss lead to changes in the facial appearance and profile.

When a person smiles, their teeth tell us all we need to know about their habits, lifestyle, and socioeconomic status. According to a poll conducted by Vision Critical a few years ago, whiter teeth are interpreted to be a sign of wealth. The survey revealed that people with whiter teeth were assumed to earn a more livable income. Their pearly whites also made them look at least five years younger than their actual age, thus improving their chances of employment by 10 percent.

The evolution of teeth presents a compelling argument that the appearance of teeth is important to our livelihood. The original purpose of teeth is still valid; however, the upkeep will affect how the world views us. Society now uses a broad brush and lumps us all together when we have missing teeth. We no longer get a pass on our teeth.

Hollywood has been sending us subliminal messages for years, and I think we are finally getting the message that in order to get the big breaks, we have to put our best teeth forward. The rich and famous will spare no expense to look their absolute best, and that means having the biggest and brightest smile. Unless our teeth are as perfect as they can be, we are hindered from putting our best foot forward. The true actor in us cannot emerge unless we are our very best self. Being our very best self means that we cannot allow our missing teeth to hold us back.

We are so far removed from the caveman. I don't think the caveman ever smiled. I know he never went to the dentist. The caveman teeth served a whole different purpose than teeth today. We don't do anything extreme with our teeth today. We simply brush, floss, and rinse, and we smile. We realize now that our teeth are very fragile and require medical attention at every stage in our development.

The evolution of teeth presents a compelling argument that the appearance of teeth is important to our livelihood. It is amazing how nature adjusts with changes in habits and culture. The caveman's teeth were big and scattered apart because of what he had to eat. Today our teeth are smaller and closer together because of the changes in the way our food is processed and prepared. Evolution dictates that nature will adjust to man and man will adjust to his surroundings so that man is always in balance with nature. The original purpose of teeth is still valid; however, its upkeep will affect how the world views us.

6

Missing Teeth
Mother Nature Insights

Since the beginning of human existence, mankind has been in a footrace with Mother Nature, mankind for survival and Mother Nature for dominance. Here are a few thoughts on the persona of Mother Nature. In order for man to be one with Mother Nature, it means to let Mother Nature have total dominance of the earth while man tries unsuccessfully to survive in a world with absolutely no shelter from rain, sleet, snow, blizzards, avalanches, tornadoes, hurricanes, erupting volcanoes, and lastly, tsunamis that rise up on the sea from the bottom caused by massive earthquakes on the ocean floor.

When we talk about missing teeth, imagine if you will, what happens in communities where thriving neighborhoods and places of business once contributed to the sounds of everyday life, then abruptly, that neighborhood and those places of businesses no longer exist. You can see the ravages of how Mother Nature comes in and over time reclaims the earth. Vacant buildings now are overrun by greenery and insects until the entire landscape changes because Mother Nature has had free reign of the earth, bringing about total devastation and repossession of the land.

The same thing happens in our mouths when we do not have a regular dental hygiene routine. The acid produced from the food we eat and the beverages we drink are allowed to have free reign of our teeth and gums. Over time, our teeth become loose and our gums get soft and infected and start to bleed. Our teeth get loose and fall out, and we are powerless to stop the process, and gradually, our mouths become a replica of an abandoned neighborhood where Mother Nature has been allowed to have free reign.

Everything man builds or constructs has to be maintained. Otherwise, Mother Nature shows up to initiate the process of chaos and destruction. There has always been a battle between man and nature. However, man's resources sometimes run out; Mother Nature never runs out of resources. A lot of cities build communities around volcanoes that lie dormant for years as if man and Mother Nature have made a truce. However, Mother Nature will break that truce and erupt, leaving man at the mercy of molten lava and blinding volcanic ash.

Man's cities and buildings are indeed built to withstand the onslaught of wind, rain, heat, and cold, but these cities have to be maintained. When people are driven out, the forces of nature are allowed to reign unopposed. This is proven evidence of cites in our communities where the citizens were driven away by tornadoes, hurricanes, tsunamis, and floods. When these communities are not rebuilt,

Mother Nature moves in with a vengeance and a thirst for dominance. Over time, she reclaims the landscape creating an entire new ecosystem.

Therefore, every time you see someone mowing the yard, trimming the hedges, and painting the house, this should be a reminder to us to brush and floss our teeth so that we can keep the ravages of Mother Nature out of our neighborhoods. Because the secret of Mother Nature is that it is a part of the natural order for things to fall apart.

MISSING TEETH

God does not discriminate
When it comes to teeth.
On the other hand,
Mother Nature might not be as sweet.
God gives each of us
A full set to use.
But some we get from Mother Nature
We might not Choose.
We use our teeth to chip, chop, and chew,
Some of these actions might not
Be wise for us to do.
The first set of teeth
Is absolutely free,
Allowing us to look and feel normal,
And just to be.
We smile and the
World smiles back.
When our teeth are missing
Our smile is offtrack.
Our teeth are not missing
In the sense of being lost.
But because we did not want to pay
The hefty replacement cost.
Mother Nature never ceases
To claim what is her own,

She comes after our teeth
From the moment we are born.
At the first sign of cavity
She goes to work,
In an effort to reclaim
All of Mother Earth.
Mother Nature and Father Time
Work hand in hand,
Everything is up for grabs
At their command.
They never stop trying to destroy
The body, mind, and teeth.
We have to be sure to brush and floss,
So our mouths don't wind up on the trash heap.
It is Mother Nature's intent to
Run wild with no laws.
Man has to be vigilant
In order to minimize our flaws,
Mother Nature's job is to
Fill empty places.
Our job is to fill the
Empty spaces.

7

"The Heart of the Author"
by Dr. Kathryn Dorn

D
r. Linda "Bobbie" Johnson has a keen eye for the physical appearance of teeth and an even keener eye for those who are secretly ridiculed, overlooked, laughed at because of it. The subject of her "heartfelt concerns" about people with missing teeth would often surface during the many conversations about issues that tugged at the heartstrings of two best friends. These conversations were therapeutic, and it led to action to encourage or help someone.

One of our conversations was about a particular lady, lady A, who worked in the church ministry in the early nineties in a small town in Arkansas. Lady A showed compassion to the choir children she worked with and was serious about her role to keep the order. Lady A had missing teeth in a pattern that one look from her, the order was maintained. There were those who would sneer about her missing teeth, but not in front of my friend. She would never be a part of jokes about people's infirmities.

My friend asked me what my thoughts were about if she would approach lady A to ask about her missing teeth. We discussed with the right heart; it would go well. At the appropriate time, the opportunity presented itself for this one-on-one conversation with lady A and my friend. Sometime later, she explained to me that lady A had a hard life with many unfortunate mistakes that caused her to lose her teeth before she turned her life around and started working at the church. Her income was very meager, and she did not have any dental insurance. During their conversation, she was prompted to ask, if she paid to replace her missing teeth, would she accept it. Lady A's response was a resounding affirmative. So quietly and discreetly, my friend asked another person with means, to go in half with her to buy lady A some teeth. She made all the dental appointments and arrangements to make this transition from missing teeth to a completed smile.

One day, my friend asked me to approach lady A to ask her a question. I did just that, and to my surprise, lady A had a perfect smile, with no missing teeth, to match her bubbly personality. Her confidence in her spoken words were sure, and her smile was strong. I returned to my friend to support and congratulate her for the secret mission, along with the help of others, that a great service had been accomplished. She later told me as a result of this kind act, lady A had gotten a better job and a new beau.

My friend's first secret support mission of missing teeth was completed. This was just the beginning of many more missing teeth projects to come. The amazing phenomena about this kind act was that my friend needed some cosmetic dental work too, that was done years later. For me, her missing-teeth concept include an array of teeth abnormalities that keep your smile shut down, your self-esteem low, and a subtle discrimination that robs individuals of some threads of self-confidence.

Our jobs ended in Arkansas, and we were transferred to similar careers in North Carolina. Working in the church there, she noticed another person whose teeth were missing. This time, she asked me to support her with paying to get this lady's teeth fixed, and we alternated paying the negotiated monthly payments. She had completed another secret mission to ward off the hidden discrimination that comes with missing teeth. My friend had become better equipped with her approach to those with missing teeth, to those who could support her with the financial aspect, and to those in the dental profession who could give a discount to help the Missing Teeth financial supporters.

One of her last Missing Teeth secret missions was to help a lady who was dating a man whose daughter and son were dentists. She felt compelled to speak to the man to have his daughter get her teeth fixed. This time, she was the catalyst to getting this lady in a position to get some help with no out-of-pocket expenses to her.

Over the years, my friend was supportive to me as I suffered bone loss and my teeth became spacy and a gap developed on my front side teeth, resembling a missing tooth. My smile was closed mouthed that looked pasted on versus a big smile with a gap that appeared on photos as a blank space. My concern when talking to others was always to speak in a fashion where my gap was not so obvious.

So self-consciously I always had double thoughts; I had to keep my professional conversations thoughts along with my missing teeth thoughts of cover-up in the same pool of knowledge.

A new dentist starting her career took me on as a client to help me get that gap fixed. She did an amazing job, and of course, she blessed me with a low financial cost to complete this project. After my missing teeth were fixed, I had my old smile back. It was amazing how I could concentrate on making the best presentations without thinking about my missing teeth.

My friend's heart of gold for Missing Teeth has been developing and growing to support others who had chronic toothaches. She provided financial support to have teeth extracted or have root canal procedures done. Her support is also protective in that she will not allow teasing another person about their teeth because she knows how damaging it is to a person's confidence. She has a keen perception of Missing Teeth and brings awareness to this growing discrimination, only to those who will support her with this cause of remedying this issue.

FINAL THOUGHTS

No matter how you use the word *discrimination*, it will not lead you to a fruitful outcome. Discrimination is so pervasive. It runs through the veins of humans, embedded in the red and blue blood that snakes its way through the veins, arteries, and capillaries.

Discrimination began the day the first slave ship landed in America from Africa. African men and women were healthy and had beautiful white, healthy teeth because of their diet. When the slave man or woman was put on the auction block, the auctioneer would parade the slave in front of the prospective buyers. The slave buyer would step up to the platform and look the individual over. He would then force the individual to open his mouth and reveal his healthy white teeth.

As part of the buying process to decide if he wanted to purchase the slave and also how much he was willing to pay for the slave, the buyer would inspect the slave's teeth. I do realize that this is a little bit of information that would not be seen by the naked eye. This is just to illustrate the importance of healthy teeth and how subtle discrimination based on the condition of our teeth has always been an issue.

With the revelation of what has been discussed in this book, will you join me in the fight to end Missing Teeth:

the last discrimination hiding in plain sight by helping another person in some small way to close the gap of their missing teeth?

BIBLIOGRAPHY

Albino, J., Baker, S., and Tiwari, T. *Reducing Oral Health Disparities: Social, Environmental, and Cultural Factors.* 2017. https://www.frontiersin.org/articles/10.3389/fpubh.2017.00298/full

Alexander, M. *The New Jim Crow: Mass Incarceration in the Age of Colorblindness.* New York: The New Press. 2010

"It May Be Smokeless, But It's Still Tobacco." Delta Dental. 2011.

Dialogue on Race Louisiana. *Original Series Participant Readings Work Book.* Baton Rouge, LA. 21, 24. 2013.

Donaldson-Evans, C. "Blinded by the White: Teeth Go Beyond Pearly." Fox News. 2016. https://www.foxnews.com/story/blinded-by-the-white-teeth-go-beyond-pearly

Gallagher, M. (2018) O'Neill Institute: Death from a Toothache: The Story of Deamonte Driver and Where we Stand Today in Ensuring Access to Dental Health Care for Children in the District. Retrieved August 4, 2019. https://oneill.law.georgetown.edu/death-from-a-toothache-the-story-of-deamonte-driver-and-where-we-stand-today-in-ensuring-access-to-dental-health-care-for-children-in-the-district/

Gavett, G. "Tragic Results When Dental Care Is Out Of Reach." Frontline. 2012. https://www.pbs.org/wgbh/frontline/article/tragic-results-when-dental-care-is-out-of-reach/

Jaffe, S. "The Tooth Divide: Beauty, Class and the Story of Dentistry." New York Times. 2017. https://www.nytimes.com/2017/03/23/books/review/teeth-oral-health-mary-otto.html

Leary, A. "How My Straight Teeth Became a Symbol of Wealth." Healthline. 2019. https://www.healthline.com/health/straight-teeth-impressions#1

Obama, M. *Becoming*. New York: Crown Publishing Company. 2018.

Otto, M. "America's Dental Health Crisis: Modern Life Causes More Tooth Decay, and Care is Increasingly Unaffordable." Common Dreams. 2019. https://www.commondreams.org/views/2019/06/08/americas-dental-health-crisis-modern-life-causes-more-tooth-decay-and-care

Paiva, M. "What Your Teeth Tell me About Your Social Class." 2015. http://www.ethnography.com/2015/09/what-your-teeth-tell-me-about-your-social-class/

Patrick, D. L. "Reducing Oral Health Disparities: A Focus on Social and Cultural Determinants." BMC Oral Health. 2006. https://www.ncbi.nlm.nih.gov › pmc › articles › PMC2147600

Polansky, B. F. "The Butterfly Effect." 2019.

https://www.dentaleconomics.com › practice › article ›
the-butterfly-effect

Rensbeger, B. and Sawyer, K. "The Challenger Report."
The Washington Post. 1986.
https://www.washingtonpost.com › archive › politics ›
1986/06/10 › challen

Sandler, A. J. "Why are Teeth So Important." 2011.
https://www.methuencosmeticdentist.com/why-are-
teeth-so-important.html

Solomon, M. "Famous Faces with Braces." 2013.
https://www.elle.com/culture/g8107/celebrities
-with-braces-faith-hill/?slide=6

Wallis, J. *America's Original Sin*. Grand Rapids: Brazos
Press. 2013.

Weeks, R. "Real Stars, Fake Teeth: 20 Celebrities Who
Have Had Cosmetic Dentistry." 2018.
https://www.more.com/celebrity/real-stars-fake-teeth-
20-celebrities-who-have-had-cosmetic-dentistry/

Wikipedia. "Tooth fairy." Retrieved July 29, 2019.
https://en.wikipedia.org/wiki/Tooth_fairy

ABOUT THE AUTHOR

Dr. Linda Johnson is a native of Shreveport, Louisiana. Her interest for chemistry began in the tenth grade and was greatly inspired by her teacher, Mr. Robert Williams, at Union High School. She would spend most of her weekends in the chemistry lab. Upon completing the eleventh grade, she earned an early admission scholarship to study chemistry at Southern University.

She is a graduate of Southern University with a bachelor of science degree in chemistry. After graduation, she went to work at Monsanto Chemical Company in St. Louis, Missouri, as a research chemist. She left Monsanto and joined the United States Army and worked for the next six years doing nuclear chemical and biological training for combat readiness.

She accepted a job at Syngenta Crop Protection as a plant chemist in North Little Rock, Arkansas. She was later transferred to the corporate office in Greensboro, North Carolina, as a regional quality specialist/internal auditor. She retired after twenty-two years and moved back to Shreveport, Louisiana.

Dr. Linda Johnson has always had a love for public speaking. Her photographic memory of reciting poems and speeches are mesmerizing to her listening audience. As a longtime member of Toastmasters International, she received the highest honor as a Distinguished Toastmaster. She uses her public speaking gift to motivate others into action—to change and improve the conditions of their lives for churches, civic organizations, colleges, and schools.

Currently she volunteers at the YWCA and facilitates Dialogue on Race Louisiana for the Racial Justice Commission. She is a member of the Flower Hill Baptist Church where she serves as the adult church school teacher and church clerk. She credits the Living Epistle Bible College for increasing her knowledge in a broad spectrum of Christian education. Her brilliance in many subjects is handled with humbleness, and she credits it all to the God whom she serves.